FOR THE CONTEMPORARY JAZZ DRUMMER
CREATIVE TIMEKEEPING

By Rick Mattingly

ISBN 0-7935-1951-9

HAL•LEONARD®
CORPORATION
7777 W. BLUEMOUND RD. P.O. BOX 13819 MILWAUKEE, WI 53213

About the Author

Rick Mattingly holds Bachelor of Music Education and Master of Music degrees from the University of Louisville, has performed extensively in jazz and rock bands, as well as with symphony orchestras, and has taught drums privately since 1970. For nine years he was an editor at *Modern Drummer* magazine, and his articles have appeared in *Modern Drummer*, *Modern Percussionist*, *Musician*, *Percussive Notes*, *Slagwerkkrant* (Holland), and *Rhythm & Drums* (Japan). He has edited instructional books by Peter Erskine, Joe Morello, Bob Moses, Gary Chester, Airto, Bill Bruford and Carl Palmer, and has served on the Board of Directors of the Percussive Arts Society.

Acknowledgements

Portions of the material in this book originally appeared in *Modern Drummer* magazine. Thanks to Ron Spagnardi for his support and encouragement of this project.

Thanks also to...
    Hal Leonard Publishing Corp.
    Grawemeyer Industries
    Peter Erskine
    and especially, Charlene, Jane and Kathryn

This book is dedicated to Theodore S. Otten

Table of Contents

Introduction

Experience shows us that life is not simply a matter of black and white or right and wrong—certainly not in the art of music. Rather, we are blessed with an infinite variety of colors and textures, as well as melodic, harmonic and rhythmic choices. The greatest challenge for a teacher in this art of music is to provide structure and discipline for a student, while at the same time giving that student a glimpse of the *infinite* musical choices possible. Rick Mattingly meets this challenge wonderfully with this book.

I've had the great pleasure of knowing Rick for many years. He has been the catalyst for many important pedagogical endeavors, including articles and Sound Supplements in *Modern Drummer* magazine, plus the highly successful Drumset Master Classes held at the annual Percussive Arts Society International Convention. He was also the editor of my book, *Drum Concepts and Techniques*.

The ride cymbal is an important topic for me; I talk about its role at some length in my book and videos, seminars and private lessons. I'm especially excited about Rick's treatment of this subject because he starts with the basics of good timekeeping and expands our understanding of **creative ride cymbal playing**. Rick has carefully explored and notated a tremendous number of rhythmic possibilities related to the ride cymbal and the rest of the kit. With care and vision, he has built upon an existing body of work related to timekeeping and coordination on the drumset (*independence*).

Creative Timekeeping sets a new challenge and fills a unique niche in the literature and teaching of the drumset. While it's possible (and desirable) to learn new musical combinations of sounds and rhythms on the kit by careful listening and practice, it is better to augment that method with a progressively graduated series of notated exercises and examples that make **musical sense**. We should all be grateful for anything that shows us such *possibilities*. I congratulate Rick for the excellence of this work, and I recommend this important book to all drummers.

Peter Erskine

Foreword

Traditionally, method books have attempted to teach jazz drumming by having students learn a single ride-cymbal pattern (ding dinga-ding dinga-ding...) and then having them play various rhythms "against" it on the bass and snare drums. Once a student can play (and read) virtually any rhythm on the bass and/or snare drum while keeping the ride cymbal pattern going, that person is said to have achieved "independence."

That's certainly a valid starting point; in fact, this book starts out the same way, which means you don't have to first go through some other jazz book before using this one. But where the other books stop, this one keeps going.

The fact is, contemporary jazz drummers do not limit themselves to that one single ride pattern. In many cases, they "break up" the time, which means that they vary the ride-cymbal pattern at will.

But what happens to the snare and bass drums? Suddenly, the "independence" ceases to exist because the repetitive cymbal pattern that it was based on is no longer there.

What has really been happening in most cases is that the drummer has learned to put his ride cymbal on "auto pilot" so that he only has to think about the bass and snare drum. But most drummers will agree that the ride cymbal is the single most important element of the drumkit when it comes to jazz timekeeping. So should that element be on auto pilot? Of course not.

Creative Timekeeping provides a variety of jazz ride-cymbal patterns as well as coordination and reading exercises that can be played along with them. The ultimate result of practicing this material thoroughly will be true independence: the ability to play *any* rhythm on the ride cymbal while playing (and reading) any rhythm on the snare and bass drums.

Chapter One:
Ride Cymbal Patterns

Part 1: Standard Ride Pattern

It is often said that jazz drummers play from the top down, while rock drummers play from the bottom up. In more concrete terms, a jazz drummer's main thrust usually comes from the ride cymbal and hi-hat, while a rock drummer is relying primarily on the bass drum and snare drum to define the pulse.

This being a jazz-oriented book, we will start with the ride cymbal. The standard swing ride-cymbal pattern, which also forms the basis of bebop drumming, is this:

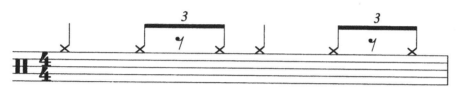

Often, you will see it notated as follows:

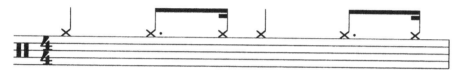

You might also see it this way:

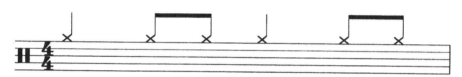

The first notation, with triplets, is the most common way to play the rhythm, even if it is notated one of the other ways. One is always expected to "swing" the rhythms when playing jazz, which basically means that you will stretch two even 8th notes to sound like the first and third notes of an 8th-note triplet, or that you will bend a dotted 8th/16th pattern to sound, again, like the first and third notes of an 8th-note triplet.

But while the jazz ride-cymbal pattern is usually played in a triplet feel, it is not always strict. Depending on the tempo, the "swung" note (the third note of the triplet) may be displaced. In a very slow tempo, it might be delayed quite a bit, so that it occurs just before the next main beat. In a very fast tempo, the swung note might be more evenly spaced between the main beats.

When first learning to play jazz, however, it is a good idea to focus on playing the ride cymbal pattern in a triplet feel. Using a metronome or drum machine set to play 8th-note triplets at a moderate speed, or simply counting triplets, play the ride-cymbal pattern along with it, making sure that each note is even.

Once you are fairly confident with the triplet feel, set the metronome to play quarters instead of triplet 8ths. When practicing the exercises in this book, it is a good idea to spend at least part of the time playing along with a quarter-note pulse on a metronome. Don't be concerned that working with a metronome will make your jazz playing sound stiff. Swing comes from the way you place the swung 8th notes, not by rushing or dragging the underlying quarter-note pulse.

If every note in the jazz ride-cymbal pattern were supposed to be exactly the same, with a perfect rhythmic subdivision and no variation in dynamics, then digital drum machines would have put all jazz drummers out of work. But that will never happen, as jazz ride-cymbal playing offers more room for personal expression than perhaps any other facet of drumming. As a result, the aspiring jazz drummer needs to devote a considerable amount of attention to developing *feel* and *touch*.

There are several different ways the standard ride-cymbal rhythm can be played:

1. every note the same

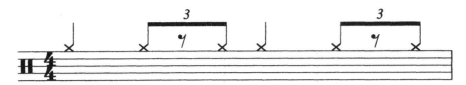

2. accented quarter-note pulse

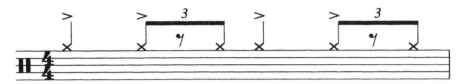

3. accents on 2 and 4

4. accents on swung notes

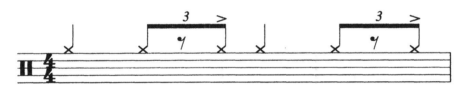

The first way is usable, but can sound a bit bland, somewhat like a drum machine. The second way is the one you should start with, as it is important to stress the quarter-note pulse. The third way is generally used only when the music is in a "two feel," which is thoroughly discussed in Chapter Four. Many drummers fall into that pattern by accident, especially because the hi-hat is often playing on 2 and 4. The fourth way should only be used in situations where you are sure the other musicians you are playing with are comfortable with it, as it is considered somewhat extreme for general playing.

Of course, written accent patterns and subdivisions are only approximations. There are endless nuances of feel and touch, and in the final analysis, how you make it feel is more important that the specific pattern you play. Elvin Jones can make the fourth pattern feel better than most people can make the first three feel.

It's very important to listen to a variety of jazz drummers in order to gain a good understanding of feel. Players such as Jack DeJohnette, Peter Erskine, Tony Williams, Elvin Jones, Max Roach, Philly Joe Jones, Mel Lewis, Joe Morello, Jimmy Cobb, Buddy Rich, Art Blakey, Louie Bellson, Danny Gottlieb, Ralph Peterson, Adam Nussbaum, Joe La Barbera and Marvin "Smitty" Smith all have great touch and feel on the ride cymbal—and each is different.

It can be helpful to play ride cymbal along with recordings of great jazz drummers. Don't worry about imitating them note for note; just try to lock in with their time feel. Ultimately, you'll find your own way.

Hi-hat
For the time being, play the hi-hat on beats 2 and 4. This is certainly not the only way to play hi-hat, but it is a very basic one, and in many situations you will be expected to do it.

Bass Drum
You want to be able to project a strong pulse with the ride cymbal alone, so you should spend a certain amount of time practicing with only the ride cymbal, with the hi-hat defining the backbeats. But you should also spend an equal amount of time practicing with the bass drum playing a straight four very softly. This can aid your overall feel by making you more aware of the quarter-

note pulse, and help you avoid unconsciously accenting the 2 and 4 on the cymbal. Also, when you are playing with a bass player who is "walking" four beats to the bar, if you can synchronize your bass drum with him to the point that you can almost imagine you are generating his notes with your foot, then the two of you will be locked in perfectly.

Note, however, that you never want your bass drum to overpower the bass. Learn to play the bass drum so softly that you can feel it more than hear it. You can always get louder if you need to, but many drummers can't get soft enough, and so they just leave it out. If you *choose* to not play bass drum, that's fine. But if you're not playing bass drum because you can't control it, that's a different matter.

Before adding the snare drum, spend some time playing the following patterns:

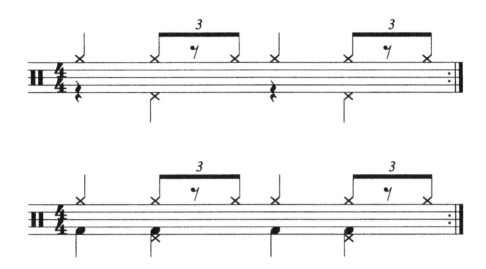

Concentrate on feel and touch. If you can't swing just playing this, then you're not going to swing when you start adding different snare drum and bass drum patterns.

Once you do feel comfortable with this basic pattern, turn to Chapter Two, Coordination Patterns and Reading exercises. Start with the Coordination Patterns. Play each one as many times as you need until it feels comfortable. The patterns should be mastered on bass drum as well as on snare drum.

When you can play all of the examples in the first group of Coordination Patterns, go to the first group of Reading Exercises. These are more "melodic" examples, most of which are based on the A-A-B-A structure that is frequently used in jazz tunes.

Once you can handle the first section of Coordination Patterns and Reading exercises on snare drum and bass drum, go to Chapter Three, which contains similar rhythmic patterns written for snare and bass combinations.

Using This Book

There are many different ways to work through this book, and students and teachers are encouraged to adapt it to their individual needs. The author does, however, encourage simultaneous practice of different sections, as ultimately you will want to be able to mix and match the various patterns and exercises in this book and arrive at a totally flexible way of timekeeping. With that in mind, do not wait until you can play the cymbal pattern in Part 1 with everything in Chapters Two and Three before beginning to practice the cymbal patterns in Part Two.

One possible method of working through the book would be to start with the basic cymbal pattern in Chapter One, Part 1 and practice it with the first group of Coordination Patterns and Reading exercises in Chapters Two and Three. Once you are ready to practice that cymbal pattern with the second group of Coordination Patterns and Reading exercises, begin to also work on the cymbal patterns in Chapter One, Part 2, along with the first group of Coordination Patterns and Reading exercises. Each time you advance to a new section of Coordination Patterns and Reading, start working on a new section of cymbal patterns with the previous Coordination and Reading exercises. You can add new cymbal patterns one at a time or a section at a time.

Besides using a metronome to assure steady tempo, you can also use it to gauge your progress. Begin each section at a slow tempo at which you can play accurately. Once you are comfortable with the basic coordination and feel, push the metronome up a notch. You might even want to keep a notebook and jot down each metronome setting as you master it. If you are working on different sections of the book simultaneously, you will also end up practicing at a variety of tempos during each practice section, which is very beneficial. There's nothing worse than a "one tempo" drummer!

Part 2: Variations

We are now going to look at variations of the standard cymbal pattern as described in the previous section. These examples only use one swung note per measure, and can be very useful when you wish to play more "open," or when the tempo is very fast.

When practicing these patterns, it is very important to concentrate on the quarter-note pulse, and avoid accenting the beat that has the swung note. Before working with the Coordination Patterns and Reading exercises in Chapters Two and Three, spend some time simply playing each of these basic patterns, with hi-hat on 2 and 4 and bass drum on a straight four. Strive for a good feel. If you can't make these patterns swing by themselves, you won't make them swing when you try to add snare drum.

It is common to suppose that the first two examples in this section are easier than the next two, because the first two are so closely related to the standard jazz cymbal pattern. But that's not always the case. When you know something well, and attempt to do something that is almost the same, the tendency is to slip back into what you already know.

Sometimes, a pattern that is significantly different from what you already know can be easier to learn than one that is practically the same. That can be the situation with patterns C and D on this page. You are not as likely to drift back into the standard pattern because these feel so different.

The point is, if it seems to take a while to get comfortable with the first two patterns, don't get discouraged and assume that the next ones are even harder. Go ahead and try them. You may find them easier. Also, the more cymbal patterns you master, the easier it becomes to learn yet another one.

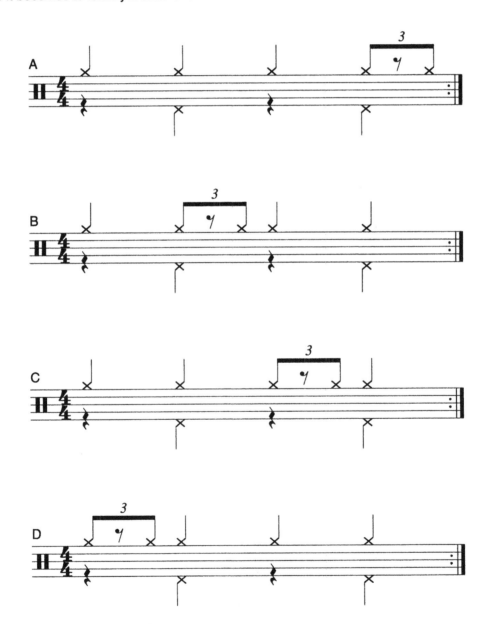

Once you can play these patterns along with the Coordination Patterns and Reading exercises in Chapters Two and Three, turn to the section titled "The Two and Four Feels" in Chapter Four to learn a very basic, but important, way to apply what you have learned so far.

The patterns below would not necessarily be used by themselves for extended periods of timekeeping; they are more likely to turn up here and there when you are "breaking up" the time by playing a different pattern in each bar. Nevertheless, the only way you can make the time feel good when you are breaking it up is by having each measure sound good within itself. With that goal in mind, you should practice each of the following patterns to the point that it feels good enough to be used by itself.

Pattern I is the one to be the most careful with in actual practice. If used repeatedly, it could sound as if you've turned the time around. But if you are playing different patterns in each measure, it could certainly be used as one of your choices.

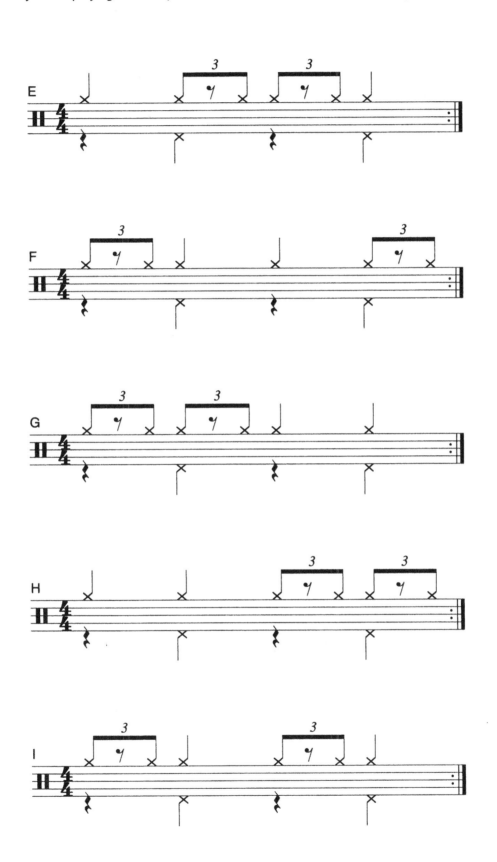

Part 3: Two-measure Patterns

The first step towards being able to break up the time at will is to get away from playing the same pattern in every measure, so this section focuses on two-bar ride patterns.

     As before, start by practicing each pattern by itself (with hi-hat and with or without bass drum), striving to make them swing. Be sure that the basic quarter-note pulse is consistent, and that you are not adding stray accents when you add the swung 8th notes. Once you have each two-bar pattern sounding good by itself, practice it with the Coordination Patterns and Reading exercises in Chapters Two and Three.

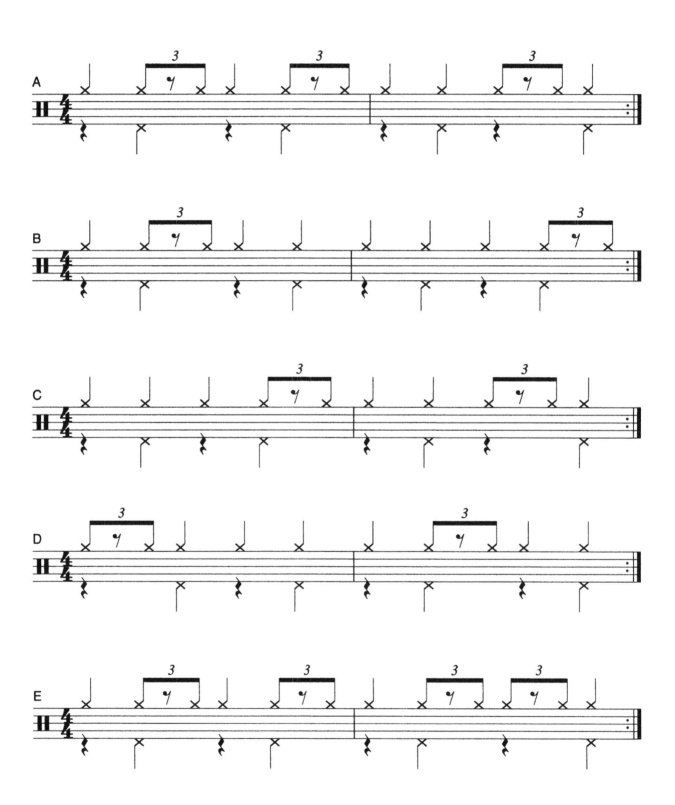

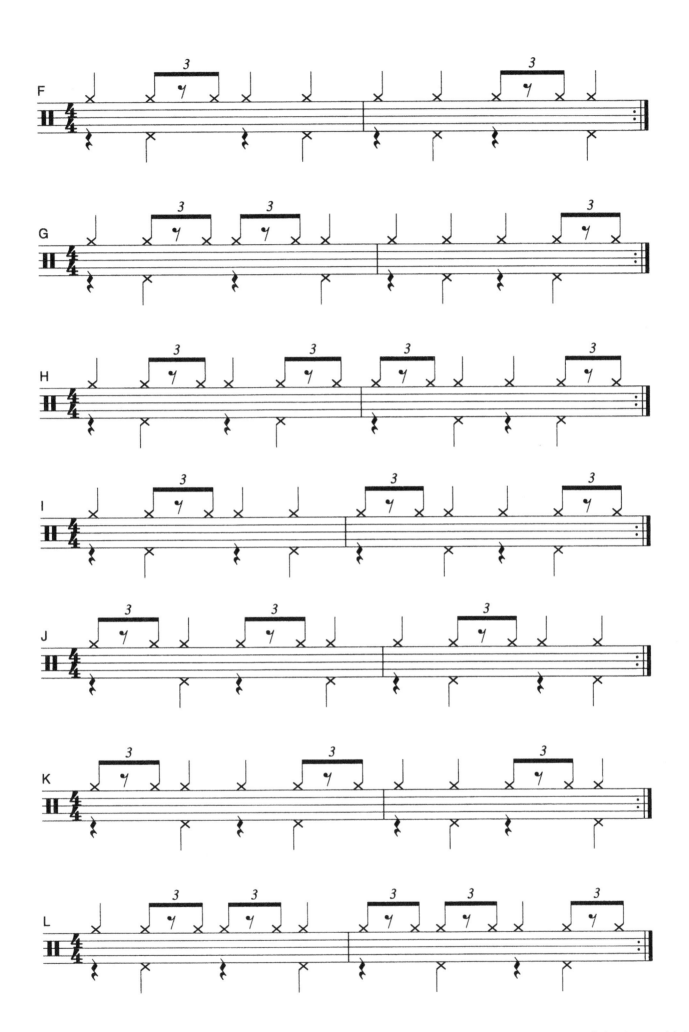

Obviously, every possible two-bar pattern is not included above. Feel free to create your own patterns, and also try combining various two-bar patterns into four-bar patterns.

Part 4: Anticipated Beats

An important facet of jazz timekeeping is being able to play "anticipated" beats, sometimes referred to as "push" beats. This is accomplished by accenting the swung 8th note and then leaving out the following on-the-beat note. The concept is illustrated in the example below, where you anticipate the downbeat of the second measure, in effect playing it "early."

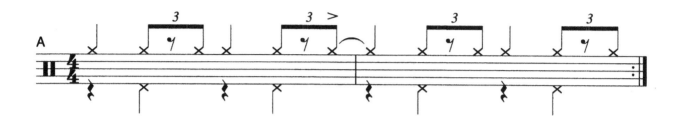

This same idea can be applied to the other three main beats in a 4/4 measure.

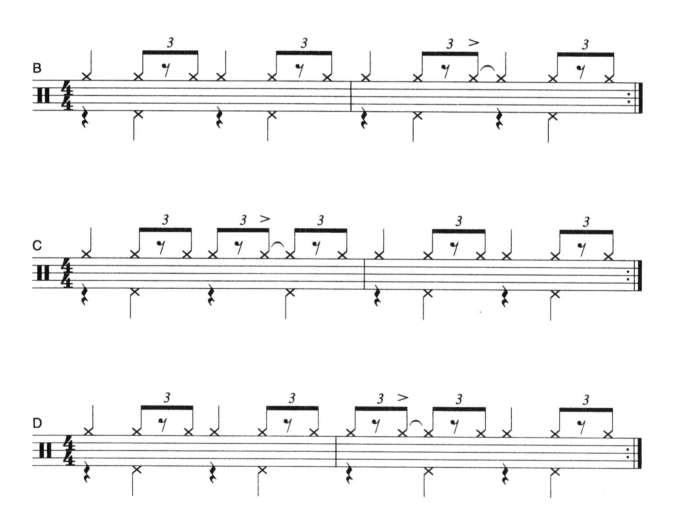

    The first four examples are based on the standard jazz ride-cymbal pattern, and are presented as two-bar patterns so that you can easily see the relationship. Obviously, the anticipated beat could be in either the first or second measure. When practicing these patterns with the Coordination Patterns and Reading exercises, you should occasionally begin with the second measure of the cymbal pattern, just to be complete.

    The biggest danger with anticipating beats is that you will play the following beat early. Therefore, when first working on these patterns, you should definitely use a metronome to keep your quarter notes consistent.

The following patterns are similar to the preceding ones, but start to get away from the standard ride-cymbal pattern a little bit. As always, there are other possibilities; these are just some basic ones to get you started towards developing a freer way of timekeeping.

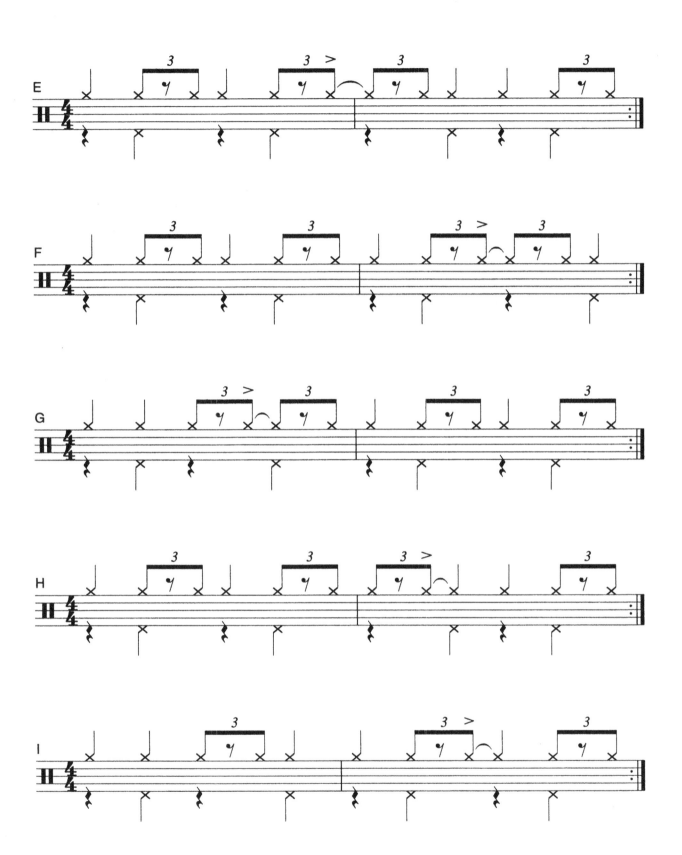

All of the anticipated beats in this section have been written with accents, as they are often played that way. But you will not always want (or need) to accent these notes, especially in situations where you are using a lot of anticipated beats. Too many accents can sometimes result in a choppy sounding time feel. Therefore, once you have mastered these patterns with the written accents, be sure to practice them without the accents, striving for as smooth a time flow as possible.

Part 5: Advanced Patterns

The following patterns fall into the "advanced" category, with most of them containing more than one anticipated beat. In order to pull these off in actual playing without confusing the other musicians or creating an ambiguous time feel, the patterns must be played with precision, and so use of a metronome is strongly advised when working them out.

Note, however, that "precision" does not have to equal "stiffness." It is entirely possible to be loose and swinging while being precise. Much of this simply depends on the quarter-note pulse being maintained. That doesn't mean that a note has to be played on every quarter note, just that whenever a note *is* played on one of the four main beats, it is absolutely in the right place. You have more leeway with the "swung" 8th notes, but you have to be especially careful when using them as anticipated beats so that the other musicians (and listeners) are never in doubt as to whether you are playing on or off the beat.

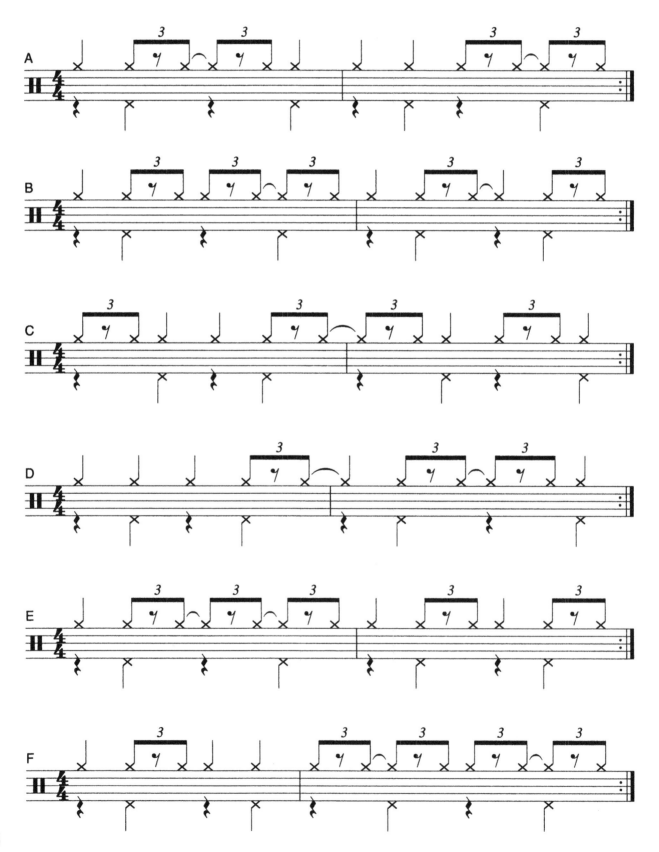

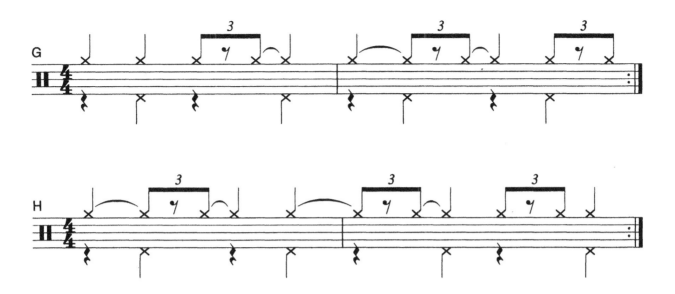

Advanced Concepts

When practicing patterns that have frequent anticipated beats, it is good to begin by keeping the other elements of your timekeeping very consistent, i.e., maintain hi-hat on 2 and 4 and play bass drum on all four beats. When working with the Coordination Patterns and Reading exercises, play everything as written.

Once you are comfortable with the feel, however, and are confident that you are maintaining a solid quarter-note pulse, you can start to adapt some of the other elements of your playing to the cymbal pattern. Ultimately, you will be able to *imply* a quarter-note pulse without always stating it.

The first step would be to anticipate the beat with the bass drum as well as the cymbal, as in the example below.

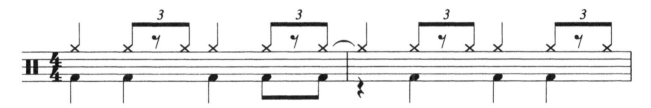

If you are anticipating the second or fourth beat, you can either anticipate the hi-hat note or leave it out.

You can also adapt the Coordination Patterns and Reading exercises to these rhythms. Note how the snare drum rhythm has been altered in the second bar to correspond with the anticipated third beat in the cymbal:

You can also adapt a pattern this way:

There are any number of ways to apply the above concepts. Remember that in jazz playing, there is seldom a single, "correct" way to approach something. Rather, there are various options to choose from. The best jazz drummers are the ones who have the most options at their disposal.

Chapter Two:
Coordination Patterns and Reading

The material on the following pages is to be used in conjunction with the cymbal patterns in Chapter One. Start with the Coordination Patterns in each section and learn to play them on snare drum as well as bass drum along with each cymbal pattern. Repeat each one as many times as necessary until it flows easily.

In many of the sections, the patterns are presented in a two-bar format. The notes in each bar are played at exactly the same time, but the two bars are written differently, with the second measure containing syncopated notation, ties, and/or dotted values.

Once you can handle all of the Coordination Patterns in a given section, proceed to the Reading exercises that follow, which are based on the previous material. Always strive for a good feel in addition to accuracy.

When working with the Coordination Patterns, don't stop when you merely reach the point at which you can coordinate them. A drum machine can do that. The point is to play each one until it is really *feeling* good. Be sure to stay with each pattern until you don't have to think too hard about your left hand or right foot and can focus most of your attention on the ride cymbal. Is it still feeling as good as it was when you played it by itself? Or, has it stiffened up a bit to match your left hand or right foot?

Remember that developing a good feel on the ride cymbal isn't enough. The way you play the snare drum and bass drum is just as important…especially in situations where the cymbal is playing a minimum of swung notes and much of the feel is being carried by the swung notes in the snare drum or bass drum.

Hint: Try playing all the rhythms in this chapter on a ride cymbal with your *left hand*. If you can't make that feel good, it's not going to be any better on a snare drum.

Finally, remember to interpret all of the 8th notes in swing style:

Coordination Patterns I

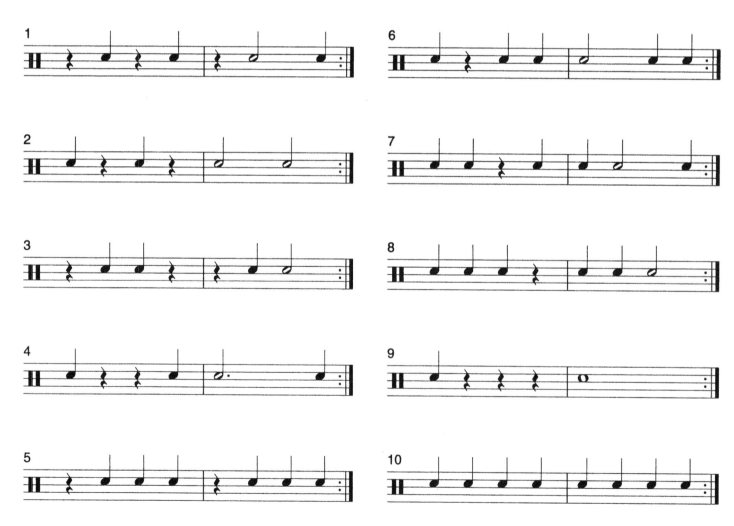

Reading I

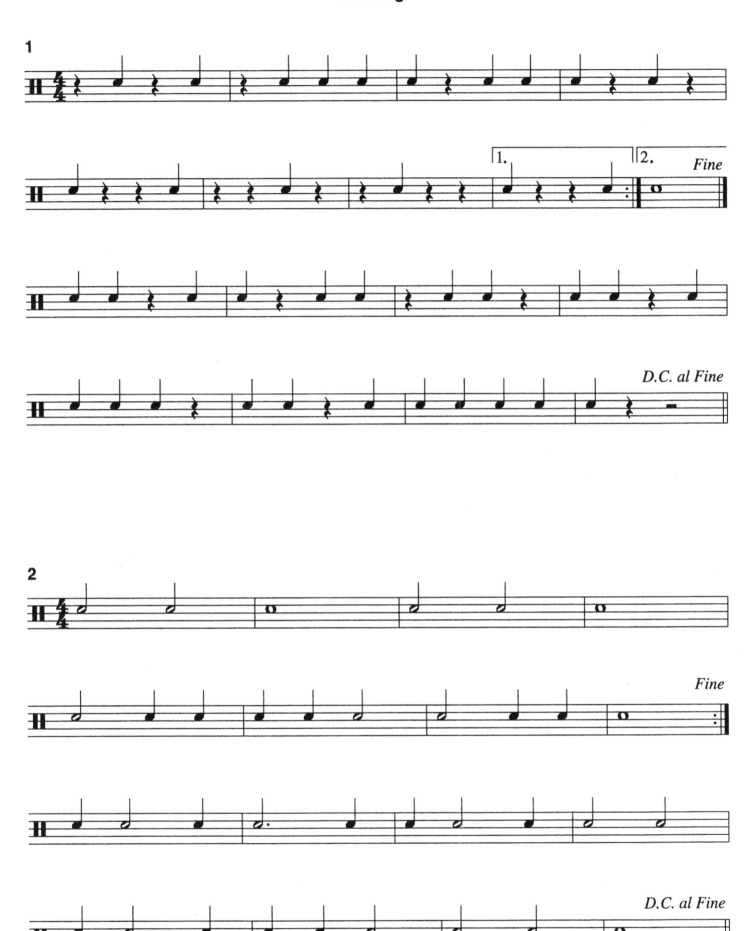

Coordination Patterns II

Reading II

Reading II

Coordination Patterns III

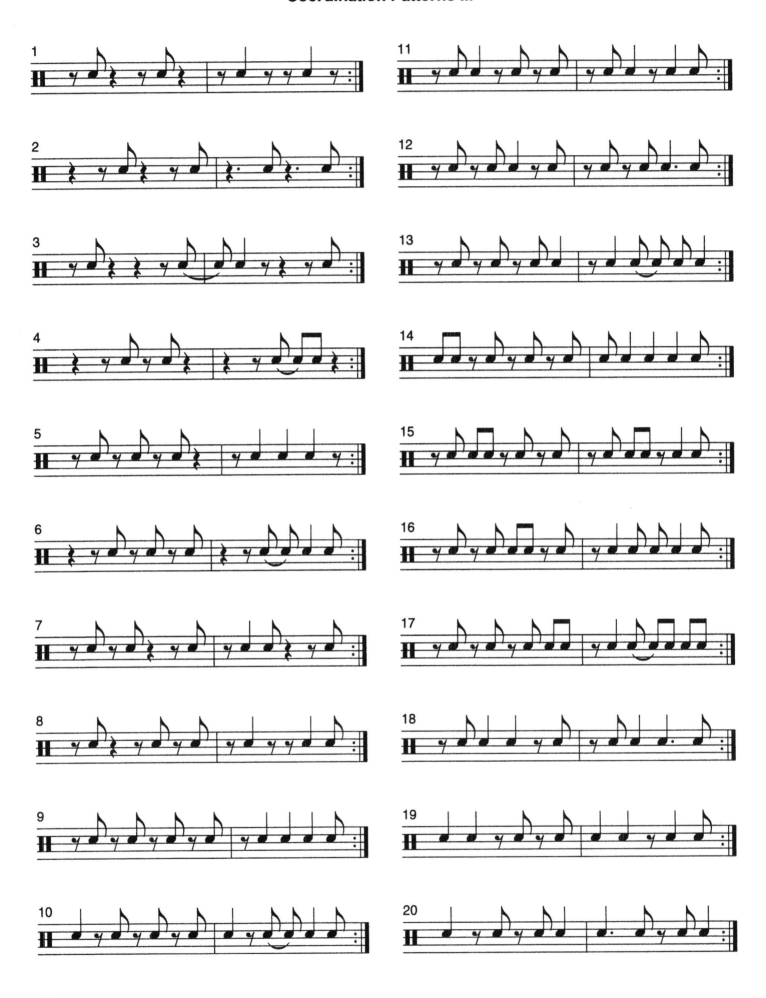

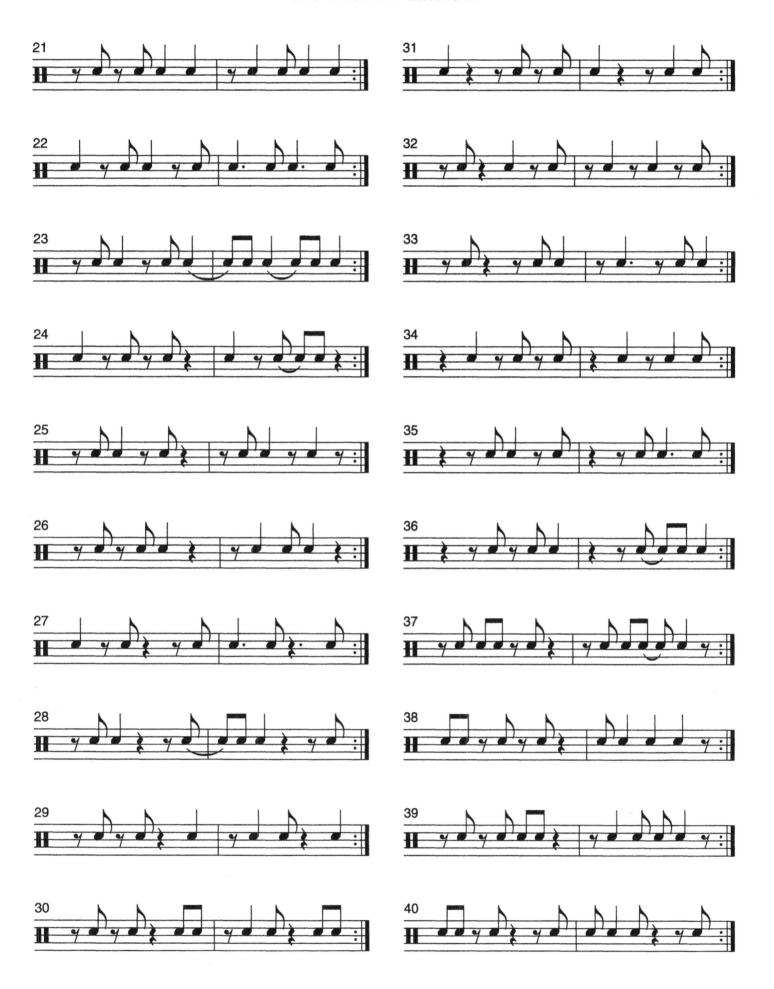

Coordination Patterns III

Reading III

1

Reading III

3

Reading III

4

Reading III

5

Coordination Patterns IV

Coordination Patterns IV

Quarter-note triplets are often misunderstood, but there is a simple way of approaching them. Think of playing every other note of 8th-note triplets, as illustrated in the example below.

Following are several coordination patterns using quarter-note triplets.

Quarter-note triplets can also be used to create an "over the barline" effect, as in the following examples. The first one illustrates the underlying 8th-note triplets.

Reading IV

1

34

2

Reading IV

3

Reading IV

Chapter Three:
Combination Patterns and Reading

This chapter contains combination snare drum/bass drum patterns and reading exercises that can be used in conjunction with the cymbal patterns in Chapter One. Before working with this material, however, be sure that you can play all of the exercises in Chapter Two on both snare drum and bass drum.

When working with the Combination Patterns, stay with each one until it is really *feeling* good. Don't settle for mere coordination; make sure that each element of the drumkit is equal in terms of feel.

Also, don't overlook the quarter-note patterns and reading exercises. They may be simple in terms of coordination, but they provide an important first step in developing the ability to split your attention between the rhythms you are reading on snare drum and bass drum and the rhythm you are playing on the ride cymbal. You should not be playing anything mechanically or on "auto pilot." Be aware of every note in terms of its accuracy and feel.

As with the previous chapter, interpret all 8th notes in swing style:

Combination Patterns I

Combination Reading I

Combination Patterns II

Combination Reading II

Combination Patterns III

Combination Reading III

1

2

3

Combination Patterns IV

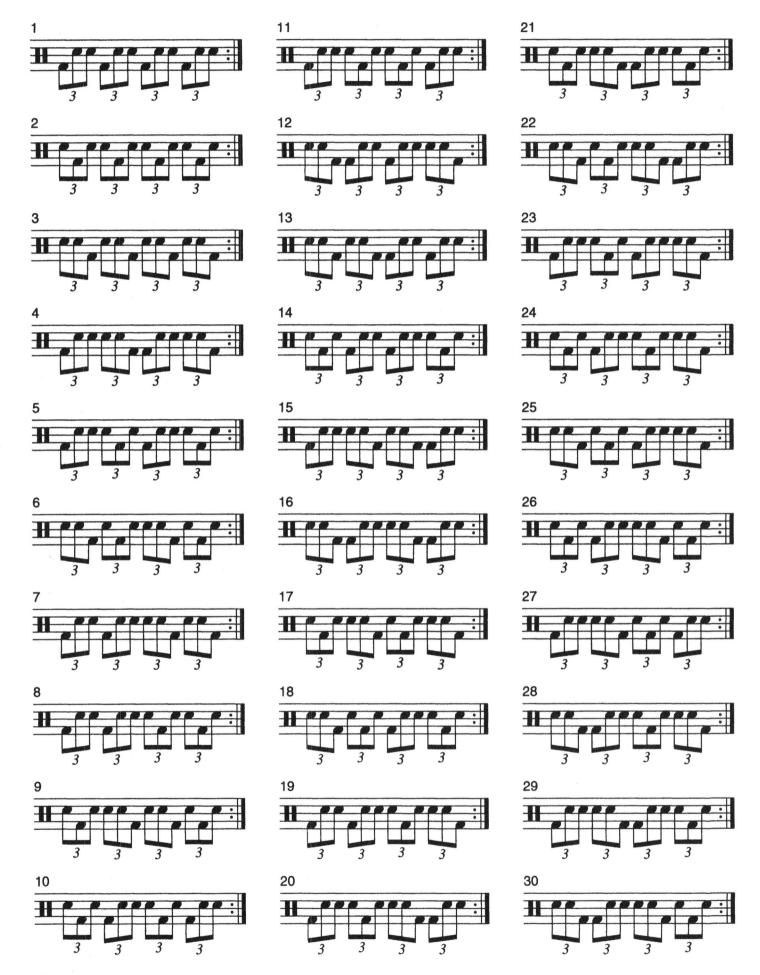

Combination Patterns IV

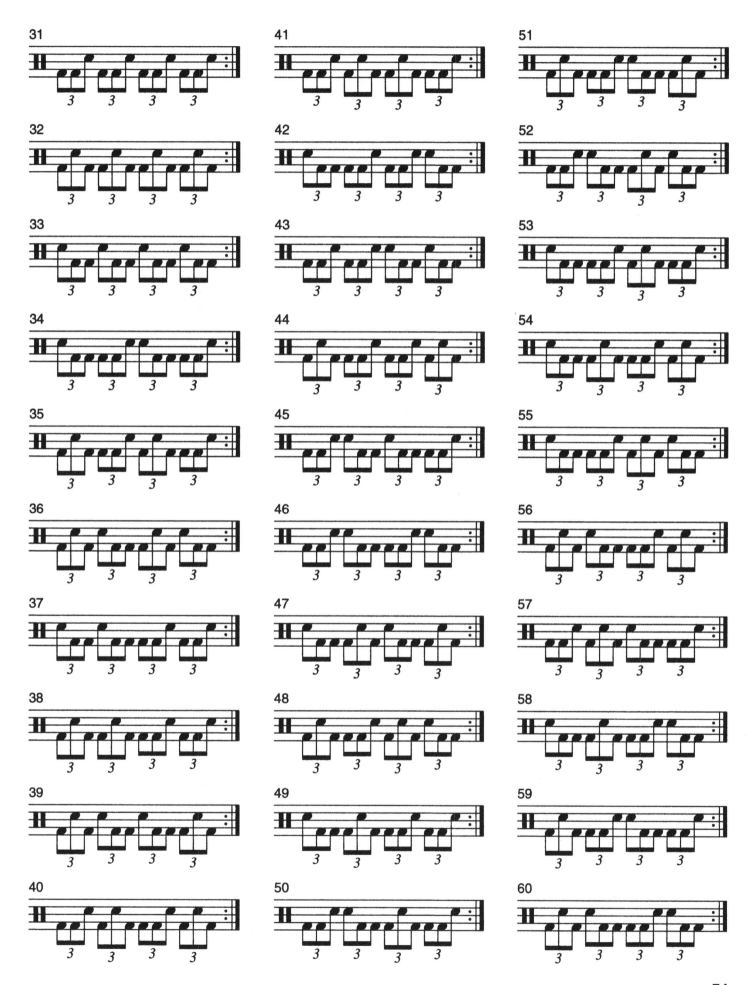

Combination Patterns IV

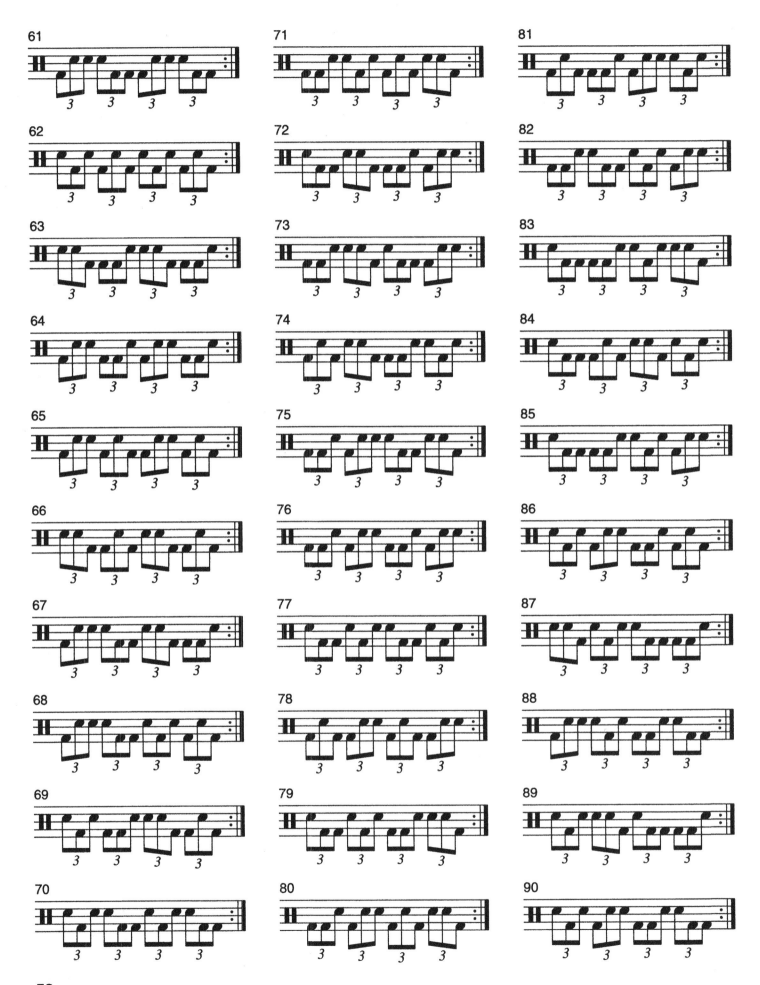

Combination Reading IV

1

2

Chapter Four:
Applications

The Two and Four Feels

In many jazz standards, the "head" of the tune alternates between a "two feel" and a "four feel." Most commonly, this occurs in tunes that are written in the A-A-B-A format. The A sections are played in two while the B section is in four.

What this means is that during the "two feel" section, the emphasis is on beats 1 and 3. Generally, the bass player will only be playing on those two beats. In the "four feel" section, there is an equal emphasis on all four beats. The bass player will be "walking" four quarter notes to the bar.

It is important for the drummer to understand the difference between these two feels and reinforce them. For the two feel, the bass drum should only play on beats 1 and 3, along with the bass player. The 2 and 4 backbeats should be emphasized, which usually means playing them on the snare drum along with the hi-hat. Generally, you will want to use the "standard" jazz ride-cymbal pattern. You can play all of the cymbal notes evenly if you wish, but it is customary to accent the 2 and 4.

The following pattern is the most basic one for playing a two feel. It is also the most effective.

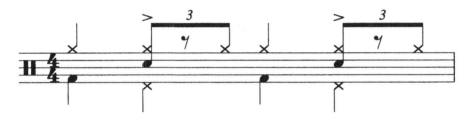

Often, for a change of color, it is customary to play the two feel on hi-hat rather than on ride cymbal. To reinforce the back-and-forth quality of the feel, the 1 and 3 are played with the hi-hat cymbals in the open position, the 2 and 4 in the closed position, and the swung notes in the half-open position.

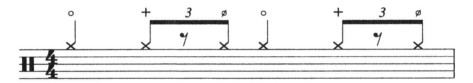

For the four feel, the bass drum plays on all four beats, and the cymbal pattern should emphasize the quarter-note pulse. You can still use the standard ride-cymbal pattern, but by no means should the 2 and 4 be accented. The basic pattern for the four feel, with the standard ride pattern, is this:

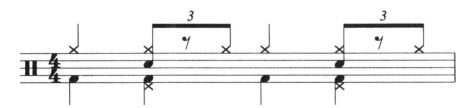

A popular technique when playing a four feel is to play a cross-stick rim click on the snare drum on 4, instead of hitting 2 and 4.

In order to emphasize the quarter-note pulse when playing a four feel, many drummers like to get away from the standard ride-cymbal pattern and play ride patterns that have fewer swung notes. You can use a repetitive pattern, such as the ones in Chapter One, Part 2, or you can break up the time at will, keeping the swung 8th notes at a minimum.

Following is an outline of a standard 32-bar A-A-B-A tune, indicating where to use the two feel and the four feel.

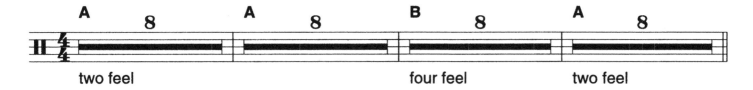

Below are some different two feel and four feel combinations. Practice them in the A-A-B-A format outlined above. Feel free to mix and match.

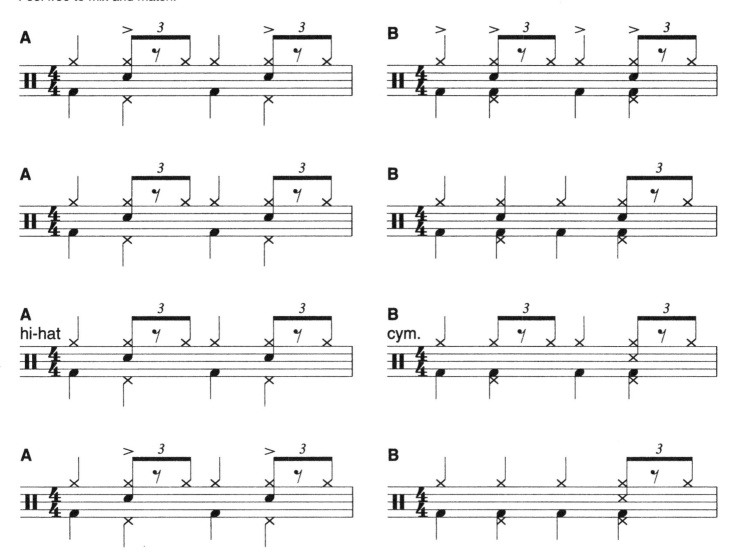

Once you are adept at changing back and forth between two and four feels, apply the above concepts to the Reading exercises in Chapters Two and Three, which just happen to be written in 32-bar A-A-B-A formats.

Double Time

Jazz players sometimes go into "double time" to add interest to a tune. In some cases, the B section, or bridge, of a tune might be played in double time, while in other situations an entire chorus may be played that way.

Essentially, double time means playing twice as fast. But it's not always as simple as simply speeding up the tempo. Often, it's just the feel that is double timed, while the overall pulse of the tune remains constant.

By way of illustration, assume that you are using the standard ride pattern for the "regular" part of the tune.

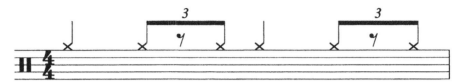

For the double-time section, you would approach the cymbal pattern as follows:

Often, even though you are doubling the speed of the cymbal pattern, you will maintain the original pulse with other elements of the kit, as in the following example:

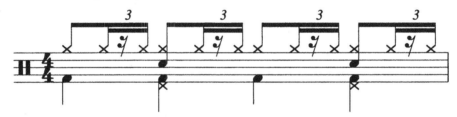

In the next example, the cymbal and hi-hat are both double-timed while the snare and bass maintain the pulse.

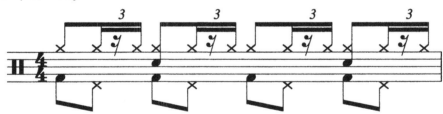

In this example, only the snare drum backbeats mark the original tempo; everything else is in the double-time feel.

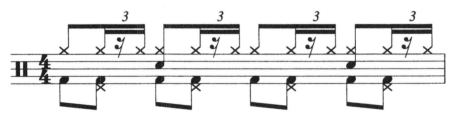

On occasion, you can double-time everything.

This concept can be applied to any of the cymbal patterns in Chapter One. Often, the patterns with fewer swung notes per bar work well for double-time sections, keeping them from sounding too cluttered. Try playing the B sections (the 5th and 6th lines) of the Reading exercises in Chapters Two and Three in double time.

Phrasing the Cymbal Pattern

Jazz drummers often have different levels of time going on at the same time. One way is to have different phrasings going on simultaneously. For example, the snare, bass and hi-hat could maintain a 4/4 feel while the ride cymbal is phrased in three above them:

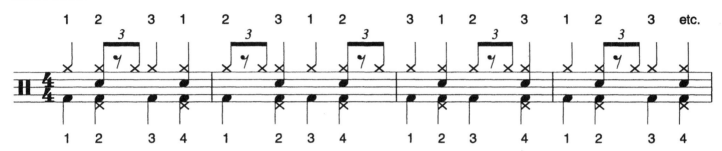

Following are some ride cymbal patterns in different phrasings. Practice them over the 4/4 reading exercises in Chapters Two and Three. Some of them, such as the patterns phrased in three, will come out even every fourth measure (in other words, the first beat of the three pattern will fall on the first beat of a 4/4 measure). Others won't come out even for quite a while. You might have to repeat the reading exercise several times to arrive at a resolved ending, or you could simply alter the cymbal pattern at the end.

Phrasings in 3

Phrasings in 5

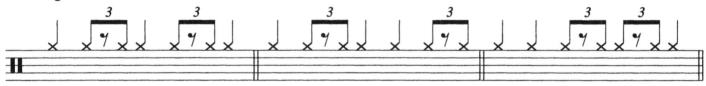

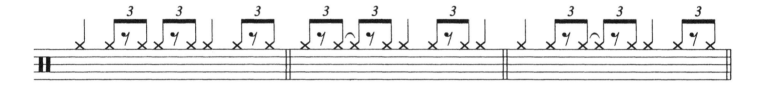

Phrasings in 7

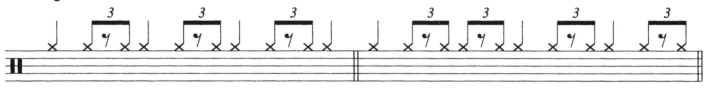

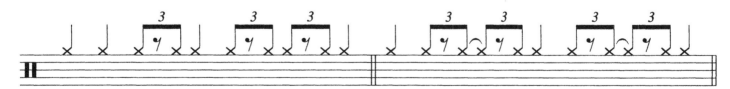

Integrating Cymbal and Snare Drum

Rather than always playing a cymbal pattern independently from the rhythms being played on the drums, some drummers prefer a more integrated approach, in which the various components of the drumset are working as one. In the example below, the cymbal pattern might appear to be arbitrary. But, in fact, it is based on a simple procedure. First, a quarter-note pulse is being maintained throughout. As for the "swung" 8th notes, they are only played when there is not a snare drum note on the "&" of the beat. This way of playing can sound less cluttered than styles of playing where the cymbal and snare drum are often sounding simultaneously, and so it is especially useful for fast tempos. Try this approach with the Reading exercises in Chapters Two and Three. (Note: for clarity, the cymbal patterns on this page have been notated with 8th notes instead of triplets, but all rhythms should be interpreted ÷swing√ style.)

An even more open way of playing is to use the "linear" approach, where the snare and cymbal are never played at the same time. In the example below, note that between the two instruments a steady shuffle rhythm is being played. Often, you will want the cymbal to be more active than the snare drum, in order to maintain the "cushion" of sound that a ride cymbal typically produces. But in certain situations it could sound good to have a more active snare drum. Also experiment with dry, pingy ride cymbals and those with a lot of sustain (perhaps one with rivets).

Of course, you don't have to fill up every beat. The following example shows an even more open way of playing. Again, this could be ideal for quick tempos in which you want to leave plenty of space for the other instruments.

When playing in the above style, it is very important that a flow is maintained between the two hands, as you can't depend on the ride cymbal alone to provide the feel. The rhythmic feel should flow between your limbs the same way a melody flows between a pianist's fingers.

60

Chapter Five:
Cymbal Reading

The following pages contain reading exercises for the ride cymbal, ranging from fairly straight ahead to a freer way of timekeeping. You can simply play these as written to get an idea of some of the ways to break up time, but it is recommended that you practice Coordination Patterns from Chapters Two and Three along with these, both on the snare drum and bass drum.

1

2

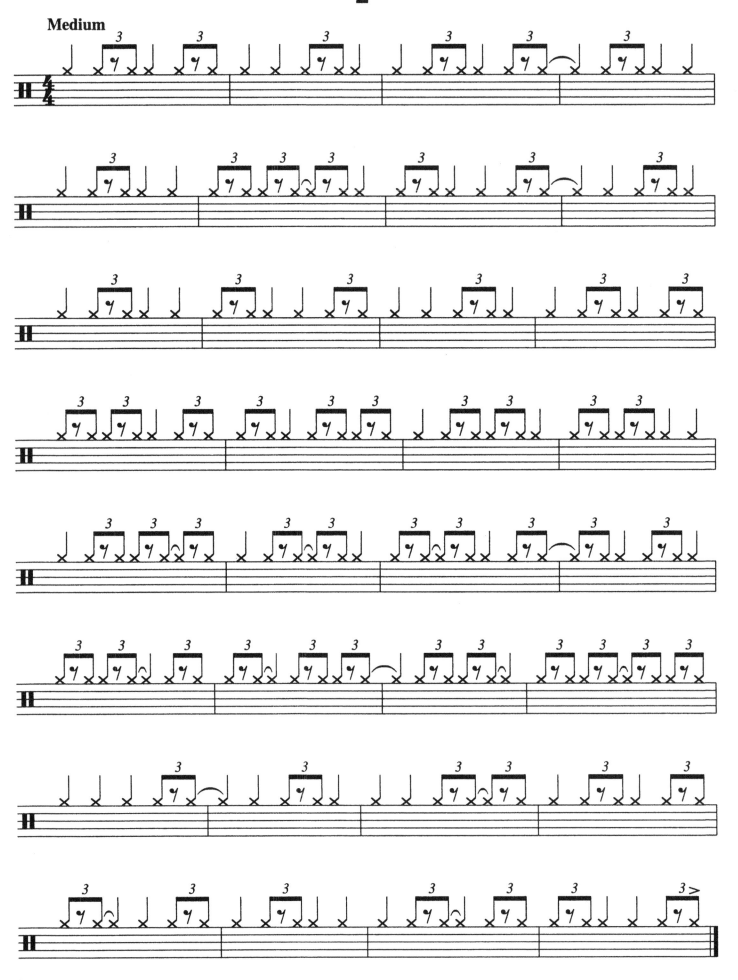

3

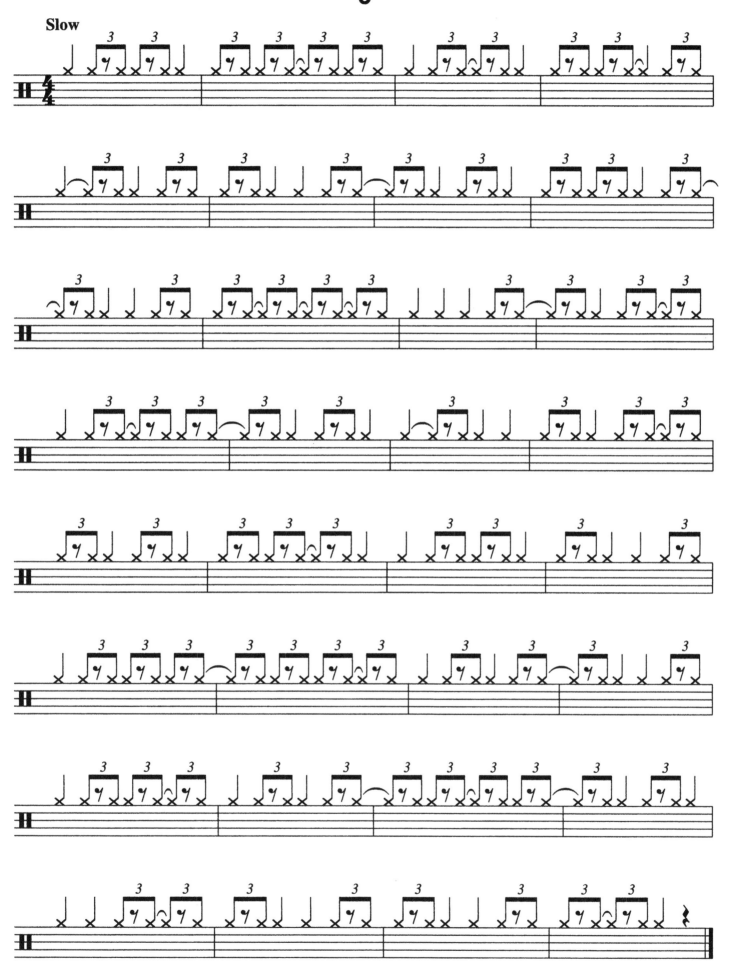

4

Medium-Fast

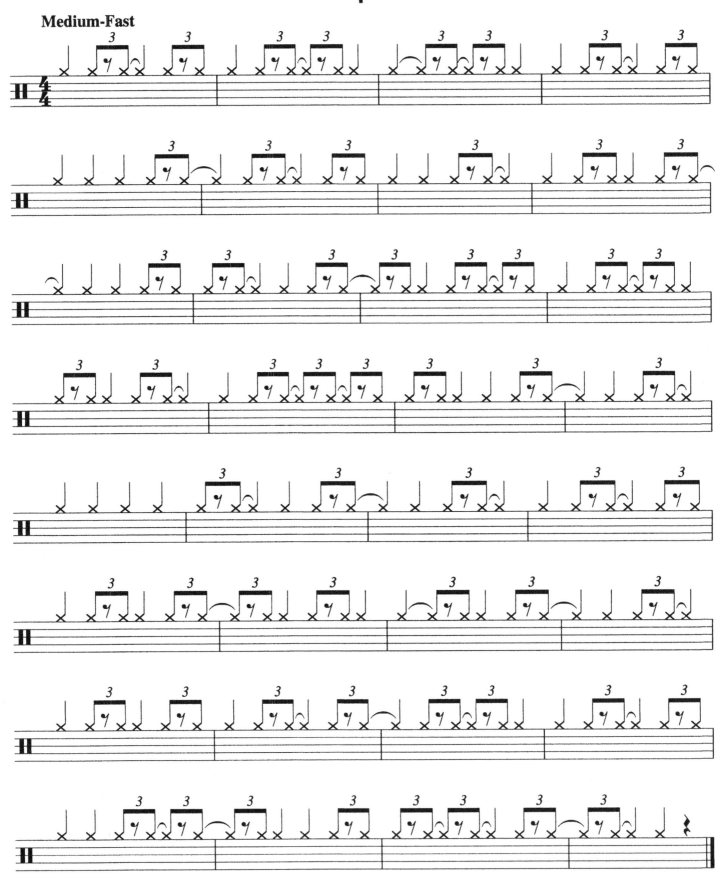

These exercises only scratch the surface of what is possible with timekeeping. While this book can help you develop a great degree of physical technique, that technique is useless if you don't have a concept of how to apply it. Listen to the masters of jazz drumming to learn different ways of playing time. But always remember that jazz is about *self* expression. Ultimately, you must find your own way.